Think Before You Crypto

Roggie Clark

Get Out of Credit Card Debt With This Book

Are you tired of living paycheck to paycheck? Drowning in interest rates and minimum payments that never seem to shrink your balance? *Understanding & Overcoming Credit Card Debt* is your roadmap to financial freedom.

https://www.amazon.com/dp/B0F3WCVWG8

Learn How To Invest in REAL Gold With This Book

Are you ready to take control of your financial future and explore the world of gold investing? Whether you're new to investing or seeking to diversify your portfolio, this beginner-friendly guide will give you the knowledge and confidence to invest in gold, and other precious metals.

https://www.amazon.com/Ultimate-Investing-Buying-Guide-Beginners-ebook/dp/B0F1KWWDXG

Learn How To Invest in Silver With This Book

In uncertain times, savvy investors turn to assets that stand the test of time-and silver, like gold, has proven itself for centuries. Whether you're approaching retirement or already enjoying it, protecting and growing your wealth is critical. The Ultimate Silver Investing & Buying Guide For Beginners is your clear, no-nonsense guide to incorporating silver into your wealth-building strategy.

https://www.amazon.com/Ultimate-Silver-Investing-Buying-Beginners-ebook

Learn Macro and Microeconomics, With This One Book

Copyright

Title: Think Before You Crypto
Author: Roggie Clark

Cover Design: Roggie Clark
Editing: Renee' Clark

Printed in the United States of America

Disclaimer

The views and opinions expressed in this book are those of the author and do not necessarily reflect the official policy or position of any individual, company, or organization cited or referenced in the text.

The author is not affiliated with any of the individuals, companies, or organizations mentioned in the text, nor does the author receive any form of compensation for citing or referencing them. Some sample scenarios in this text are fictitious. Any similarity to actual persons, living or dead, is purely coincidental.

The professional information (strategies, tips, and concepts) in this text is provided on an "as is" basis, without warranties of any kind, express or implied. While every effort has been made to ensure the accuracy of the information contained herein, neither the author nor the publisher makes any representations or warranties regarding its completeness, reliability, or applicability. The information is for educational and informational purposes only and should not be interpreted as professional, legal, financial, or business advice.

This book does **not** constitute financial advice, investment guidance, or legal counsel. Any financial, business, or investment decisions made based on this book are done **at your own risk**. You should always conduct your own research and consult a **certified financial**

advisor, legal professional, or other qualified expert before making any decisions that could impact your finances, business, or legal standing.

Neither the author nor the publisher guarantees any specific results or outcomes. By reading this book, you acknowledge and agree that the author and publisher shall not be held liable for any direct, indirect, incidental, or consequential damages, financial losses, or harm arising from the use or misuse of the information contained in this text. You assume full responsibility for any actions taken based on the content of this book.

Table of Contents

Chapter 1: The Hype Train

Let's start with what you know. Cryptocurrency is everywhere. You've seen the headlines, the flashy Instagram stories, the crazy TikToks, and you've heard influencer after influencer mention it. Maybe you even have a friend who swears they bought into Bitcoin early and now lives in a mansion. Stories like that dominate the internet.

Crypto is presented as the golden ticket to financial freedom—a new way to pay for everything. Hell, there are investors calling it "digital gold" - like it's supposed to be better than owning the real metal! Essentially, the rhetoric is that crypto is the future of a better life.

Now I hope that when you heard all the "success stories" and saw the hype train coming, and thought to yourself - "this is too good to be true." You are right. Here's the truth. Despite all the miracle stories you've heard, most people do not get those kinds of astronomical returns with crypto. I mean, sure, on average, if you time the market right, you can make some money as a novice, but to make it big, you've got to have the time, capital, and know-how to do it.

So, no disrespect to the people who do make lots of money with crypto, but most have lost thousands (if not more) on memecoins that never took off, or worse, on scams that drained their wallets. But the winners? The creators of the coins and the exchanges that sell them. They get the spotlight. They're the ones doing podcasts and giving presentations. They're the ones whose faces are on the front of magazines. Crypto's hype train runs on those stories.

Take a look at the numbers. Over $1 trillion has been invested in cryptocurrencies globally. In 2021 alone, Bitcoin surged from under $30,000 to over $60,000 (CoinMarketCap), riding a wave of FOMO (fear of missing out). Social media is flooded with every influencer trying to sell you the "next big thing" in crypto. Their pitch? "Get in now, or you'll miss out on the next 100x return." Even investment firms are starting to sell seniors on putting their retirement savings into crypto.

Again, they sell to you that this is a "once-in-a-lifetime opportunity." But what no one's telling you is the other side. The side where most people lose money. The side that isn't advertised. The side that's buried under the shine of cars and beach vacations.

The truth is, most people don't see the downside until it's too late. When the market is booming, it's easy to get swept up in the excitement. But when the market crashes—like it inevitably does—you're left holding a bag of worthless coins with the stupid advice of an influencer in your ear who said "buy the dip."

The same coins you thought would make you a millionaire are now just digital garbage, just sitting there. This isn't just a possibility, it's a commonality for many investors. When things go south, they're often left with no recourse. There's no safety net, no insurance policy. You can't call up your bank and ask for your lost money back.

Crypto isn't some quick fix or shortcut to wealth. For every person who strikes it big, there are thousands who are left with empty pockets. Now I am not saying don't try it, I just think it is time for the crypto bros to start being more honest.

So before you jump in, ask yourself: Is this really a smart decision? Are you prepared for the possibility that you might lose everything? Because in the world of crypto, that's the cold, hard truth that no one tells you about.

In this book, we are going to go into more detail about crypto investing, so you can decide for yourself if it is really worth your time. Better to have spent a little bit of money on this book than to have to endure thousands in losses. Think of this book as your seatbelt, so let's buckle up and dive in.

Chapter 2: The Questions We Need to Ask

Let's take a moment to reconsider the big picture. If crypto is as amazing as it's made out to be, why does it take so much knowledge, skill, and know-how to make money right away? Like, why does it seem like you need some sort of cheat code or special ability to even get a couple of dollars? Shouldn't you be able to get in right away and see success?

I mean, of course, you should take the time to do your research and get acclimated to how the markets and the tech works, nothing in life is free – we get that. But let's get past the motivational speak. Why does it take so much work to make a little bit of money?

And of course, the real knitty gritty gets no attention, but all the stories of crypto millionaires, and thumb drives lost in the county dump that apparently have all these crypto dollars on them. We've heard it, for some reason, those stories get all the attention. But how many of those winners got in early? How many perfectly timed their entry and exit? How many were seasoned investors with a deep understanding of the market? For most people, the success stories sound like pure luck. And that's the part no one wants to admit.

Timing, knowledge, and not luck—but insider information are the real factors that separate the small number of winners from the rest of the crowd. The majority of people in crypto end up holding onto coins that lose value, hoping they'll recover, but often, they never do. Most people believe they can make a quick profit, but the market doesn't work that way. Getting in at the right time, having the right insight, and understanding when to pull out are all crucial parts of the game. And of course, a little bit of insider info, but apparently that's a dirty secret, but it happens more than you think.

That's why we need to ask these tough questions before promoting the world of crypto. These are the kinds of questions that don't get asked enough, yet they could have saved countless people from losing money. One of the first questions is simple: How many people actually make money with crypto?

The reality is that the vast majority of people do not. A report by the FBI indicates that Americans lost $5.6 billion in cryptocurrency fraud schemes in 2023 alone, highlighting the significant financial risks involved (FBI). So you are essentially risking your hard-earned money on a system that is full of risks.

Next, let's consider this: What happens to those who don't sell at the peak? The simple answer is a lot of regret. The volatility inherent in cryptocurrency markets means that prices can fluctuate wildly, leading to substantial losses for investors who fail to time the market correctly. For instance, in 2024, phishing attacks emerged as the most costly security threat in the crypto industry, resulting in over $1 billion in stolen digital assets across 296 incidents (CertiK).

And let's not forget the biggest question of all: Who's making money from your excitement? It's not the average person buying and holding coins. Instead, it's the people who sell you the dream.

The creators of fraudulent tokens and the platforms facilitating these scams are the ones profiting the most. In 2024, more than half of all new crypto tokens launched were deemed malicious, showing how rampant fraudulent schemes in the market are (CoinDesk). This dynamic is something most people don't consider when they dive into crypto. Now, there are definitely platforms that are safer, but let's be clear, there are far more FTXs than there aren't – just saying.

Everyone is so focused on the potential rewards that they forget about the people profiting off their excitement. It's not about helping you become a millionaire; it's about selling you a vision, and in the end, it's their pockets that get lined. In an annual report from Immunefi on the crypto ecosystem, they noted that the crypto industry lost $1.49 billion in 2024 due to hacks (Immunefi). So you can't just trust any platform you see online.

There's also something else we need to address when we talk about the small number of winners in crypto.

Many of these so-called “winners” didn’t just get lucky; they knew exactly what they were doing.

These individuals or companies had insider knowledge, a strong network, and resources to weather the volatility that crushed the average investor. The reason they were able to succeed was not because crypto is some magical wealth machine, but because they approached it with a calculated strategy, knowledge, and preparation. A report by Chainalysis indicates that high-yield investment scams and pig-butchering scams accounted for around 50% and 30% of losses in 2024, respectively, revealing the sophistication of fraudulent operations (Chainalysis)

Before you think about jumping into crypto, ask yourself if you’re truly ready to deal with the risk. Are you prepared to handle the wild swings? Do you have the knowledge to recognize a scam before it drains your wallet? Can you afford to lose what you’re about to invest?

These are questions that should be at the forefront of your mind, but they often get overlooked in the excitement of the chase. The people who profit most in crypto are those who understand the risks and know when to step back. If you’re just hoping for a quick payday, you’re more likely to fall victim to the hype—and the ones making money from it.

Chapter 3: The Reality Check – Hard Data and Cold Truth

Let's dig in a bit further and talk about how incredibly unpredictable crypto can be. A coin's value can skyrocket by 100% one day, only to drop by 60% the next. This isn't financial freedom. This is closer to gambling, where the highs are addictive, but the lows can wipe out everything you've invested. It's that volatility that catches so many people off guard, leaving them with nothing to show for their excitement and hopes of getting rich.

The hard truth is that most people lose when it comes to crypto. According to a report from Bank of America, a staggering 82% of crypto investors end up losing money. That's a huge majority of people who enter the market thinking they're going to make a quick buck, only to find themselves with empty wallets and regrets (FTC).

Like I said, in Chapter 1, crypto's promise of big returns is rarely paired with a much darker side—the side that doesn't get shown in those influencer-driven success stories. People are constantly told they can "make it big," but they're rarely told about the risks and pitfalls that accompany those dreams.

The most common mistake? **FOMO**, or **fear of missing out**. It's what drives so many people to buy at the highest point, only to panic sell when the market dips. It's the same thing that causes people to run up a credit card, and the same thing that leads to a crypto debt trap waiting to happen. This cycle of buying high and selling low is what destroys most investors. "Buy the dip" is one set of words that's a highway ticket to a broke bank account.

You cannot react emotionally when investing, you have to make strategic decisions based on a solid understanding of the market. In the end, the people who lose out are the ones who let their excitement drive their actions, not their knowledge.

Now, you might be thinking, "But wait, that's not right, what about all the people who did make money?" But here's the thing: the majority of people who profit from crypto are those who got in early, understood the technology behind it, and knew what they were doing. Most of them took calculated risks, and yes, many had insider information.

They didn't just jump into the latest meme coin hoping for the best. They had a plan, they researched, and they made informed decisions. People like Elon Musk, Mark Cuban, Satoshi Nakamoto (who might be the creator of Bitcoin), and others knew about cryptocurrency from the beginning, and definitely had a part in making it what it is today. So I am sure it is in their and other crypto bros' best interest to tell you how great it is, but unfortunately, I just keep finding that they spend more time on the hype and less on the real – the "real" is what keeps you from losing everything.

If you're still sitting there thinking, "I could be one of the lucky ones," let me tell you from personal experience—crypto is not a quick fix or some magical formula to wealth. Trust me when I say this: there's no cheat code. Without a clear understanding of the market, you're not investing—you're gambling. And more often than not, gambling leads to loss.

So, before you dive headfirst into crypto, take a step back and think. Ask yourself if you're prepared for the unpredictable ride. Or are you just chasing the dream that seems a little too shiny to be true? The reality is that the odds may be stacked against you, and the stories of success don't always tell the whole truth.

Chapter 4: The Hidden Dangers – Scams, Fraud, and the Dark Side of Crypto

I've talked a little bit about crypto scams and fraud in Chapter 1, but honestly it's so damn rampant that it needed it's own chapter. While crypto is often presented as an innovative and exciting financial frontier, it's also a breeding ground for bad actors. The anonymous nature of digital currencies, which can be one of their strongest selling points, is also what makes them ideal for scammers looking to exploit the unwary. Fake projects, pump-and-dump schemes, rug pulls, and exit scams are all too common in this space.

In fact, over $40 billion has been lost to fraud in the crypto market in just the past five years (Hughes, 2023). That's not pocket change. It's a staggering amount of money, much of it belonging to regular investors who thought they were getting in on the next big thing. These scams are often dressed up in shiny packages—promises of huge returns, "guaranteed" profits, and "unbeatable" investments. Unfortunately, the promises rarely match reality, and once the scam artists have their hands on your money, it's gone.

But it's not just the small-time, fly-by-night schemes that pose a threat. Even the most well-known and established coins haven't been immune to fraud and security breaches. Take Bitcoin and Ethereum, two of the largest and most known cryptocurrencies in the world.

They've both seen massive amounts of funds lost due to poor security practices, hacking, and vulnerabilities within exchanges and wallets. Investors may think they're safe by sticking to the popular coins, but the truth is, the crypto market is riddled with opportunities for fraud at all levels (Smith). I mean, c'mon, Bitcoin was invented to be used as an untraceable currency by people who do illegal things – so knowing that alone, don't be surprised that the fraud and scams are common.

And to make matters worse, it's not always easy to spot a scam. Fraudsters are experts at using slick marketing tactics and FOMO to convince people to part with their money. One of the most common tactics is the "**pump-and-dump" scheme**, where a group of people artificially inflate the price of a coin to attract new investors, only to sell off their holdings once the price is high enough, leaving newcomers with worthless coins. This kind of manipulation can happen quickly and without warning, and if you're not paying attention, you could easily fall victim.

Exit scams are another troubling phenomenon in the world of crypto. In these cases, creators of a cryptocurrency or project will attract investors with promises of high returns, only to suddenly vanish when the money is raised, taking everything with them. By the time the investors realize they've been scammed, it's often too late to recover their funds. These types of fraud have been all too common in the crypto world, with new scams popping up regularly. The anonymity and lack of regulation in the market make it extremely difficult to hold anyone accountable (Carter).

So, how can you protect yourself? The first step is simple: be skeptical. Stop taking every damn thing for face value. If something sounds too good to be true, it probably is! Always do your research, and don't be afraid to walk away from projects that raise red flags. Make sure you understand the risks involved before you commit your money, and never invest more than you can afford to lose. Trust your gut—if you feel like you're being rushed into a decision, that's usually a sign that something is off.

Investing in crypto is risky enough without adding fraud and scams into the mix. While the potential for high returns can be enticing, it's important to remember that the road to success is littered with potential pitfalls. If you're serious about investing, you need to understand the dangers, stay informed, and approach the market with caution. Don't let the allure of easy money blind you to the very real risks that exist. In the world of crypto, the price of ignorance can be steep, and it's a price that far too many have paid already.

The truth is that as long as the crypto market exists and as long as anonymity reigns, fraud will continue to be a significant threat. The lack of oversight makes it harder for investors to differentiate between legitimate opportunities and fraudulent schemes. Without clear regulations and protections, it's easy for bad actors to thrive while the average investor gets left behind.

Chapter 5: The Legal Side of Crypto – What You Need to Know

Like I said, the world of crypto is still largely unregulated. Despite its explosive growth, the legal landscape is struggling to keep up, leaving investors exposed to risks they might not even be aware of. The truth is, stepping into the crypto space without understanding the legal implications is like gambling with your financial future.

One of the first things you need to understand is how taxes work with crypto. Many people assume that because it's digital, crypto transactions are somehow free from taxation. But that's far from true. Depending on where you live, you could owe capital gains tax on your profits. Failing to report your gains could lead to penalties. Now I know the Internal Revenue Service is quickly becoming a relic of the past, but still, just be conscious of the fact that crypto could be taxed like all other investments.

Then there's the risk of government intervention. What happens if the government decides to regulate or even ban certain coins? It's not as far-fetched as it sounds. Countries like China have already implemented strict bans on crypto, and other nations are considering similar measures. If the government were to suddenly outlaw your investment, it could lead to financial losses or even legal trouble. You could find yourself holding onto assets that are no longer recognized as valid or valuable. This potential for sudden shifts in policy adds a level of uncertainty that you just don't get with more traditional investments.

Operating in a legal gray area is another huge risk many overlook. Crypto transactions are often anonymous, and there's little oversight on many exchanges. This opens the door for illegal activities such as money laundering, which could lead to legal action against individuals involved, even if they didn't intentionally break the law. Just because something is legal today doesn't guarantee it will remain that way. Regulations could change overnight, and if you're caught in the wrong situation, the consequences could be devastating.

With these factors in mind, it's clear that you need to take the legal side of crypto seriously. Before making any investments, make sure you understand the potential risks—whether they're related to taxes, future regulations, or possible legal issues. Only by educating yourself on these matters can you avoid falling into a trap that could cost you everything.

Crypto might offer enormous rewards, but without a strong understanding of the legal landscape, those rewards come with heavy risks. Proceed cautiously, be prepared, and always ensure you're on the right side of the law before you invest your hard-earned money into digital coins.

Chapter 6: The Psychology of Crypto – Why We Keep Falling for It

Even with all the scams, fraud, and uncertainty, people still keep pouring their money into crypto. So why do people keep doing it, despite all of the risks? Let's look at the psychology of the average crypto investor. For one, they clearly enjoy the idea of **instant gratification**. The desire for quick success triggers our natural instincts to chase after big rewards. It's like a dopamine hit to them. When the value of a coin spikes, it feels like the universe is finally on their side. But when the value drops, the feeling of devastation can be overwhelming. This emotional push and pull can cause them to make decisions that they would otherwise never make, all driven by the hope of recovering from the loss (Hobson).

Like I said in the last chapter, **fear of missing out**, or **FOMO**, also plays a huge role in these decisions. It's the reason people jump into a market without fully understanding it, just because everyone else seems to be making money. They see others getting rich, and suddenly, the fear of being left behind takes over their logic, causing them to jump in headfirst. (Gabbrielli).

Then there's **confirmation bias**. This is when people ignore the warning signs and only seek out the positive stories about crypto. They ignore the potential for failure and instead focus on the handful of success stories that dominate the media. It's easy to believe the hype when you're only looking for things that support your beliefs, and this can keep people locked in the cycle, unable to make clear-headed decisions (Anderson & Kwan).

Another common psychological trap is **loss aversion**. Again, like I said, when people start losing money, they often become more desperate to recover it. Instead of cutting their losses, they double down, thinking that if they just put in more money, they'll be able to fix the situation. This only amplifies the losses, creating a never-ending loop of poor choices (Mullins).

The truth is that investing in crypto isn't about logic. That's not what the creators had in mind – for them, they keep it going to drive your and others' emotions. They know the high you feel when your account balance climbs and the crushing feeling when it drops. They know you can be easily manipulated and become addicted to it. The powers that be know this, hence the reason crypto keeps getting so much media coverage.

But here's the bottom line: If you don't keep your emotions in check, you'll make decisions driven by fear, greed, and pride, instead of rational thought. And in the age of Aquarius, those decisions will not end well.

What makes crypto all the more of a gamble is how easily emotions can cloud your judgment in such a volatile market. People tend to overlook the need for proper research, risk management, and the importance of setting clear financial goals. Instead, they get caught up in the thrill of the chase and focus on short-term gains rather than long-term strategies. That's why it's crucial to step back and ask yourself: Am I making this decision because it's a smart investment, or because my emotions are driving the choice?

In a world that values quick results, crypto promises a shortcut to wealth. However, the real wealth comes from knowledge, patience, and strategy. Without these, you're not investing—you're gambling, and that's a game where the house often wins.

So, as you can see, there's a lot of psychology that goes into why people invest in crypto. This is why I think it is so important to really practice **metacognition** and to ask yourself why you are investing in crypto, and what you truly are looking to gain from it. Now's not the time for the whimsical dreams; be really serious about what you want to get out of it, and that, my friend, is the key to success in investing.

Chapter 7: The Cost of Crypto – Fees, Mining, and Hidden Expenses

Along with the legal stuff and taxes involved with crypto, another often overlooked aspect in the crypto world is the associated costs. While the potential for substantial profits is frequently highlighted, the expenses can accumulate rapidly.

Transaction Fees

Every crypto transaction incurs fees, whether buying, selling, or transferring. These fees vary across different cryptocurrencies and platforms. For example, Bitcoin's average transaction fee surged by 900% over a three-month period in 2023, reaching approximately $15.65 per transaction (Bankless Times). Similarly, Ethereum's average transaction fee stood at $2.41, highlighting the cost disparities among various cryptocurrencies (YCharts).

Mining Expenses

Mining cryptocurrencies, especially Bitcoin, entails significant energy consumption. Bitcoin's annual energy usage is estimated at around 127 terawatt-hours (TWh), surpassing that of countries like Norway (Buy Bitcoin Worldwide). A single Bitcoin transaction can consume up to 1,200 kilowatt-hours (kWh) of energy, which is nearly equivalent to 100,000 VISA transactions (Buy Bitcoin Worldwide). This immense energy demand contributes to environmental concerns and adds to the operational costs of mining activities.

Security Costs

Protecting your crypto assets requires investing in secure wallets. Hardware wallets, designed for enhanced security, can be costly. Even less secure options still incur transaction fees when moving coins, adding another layer of expense (GOBankingRates).

Exchange and Account Fees

Storing crypto on exchanges often involves withdrawal or conversion fees. Additionally, some platforms impose annual fees on certain crypto accounts, which can erode profits over time.

These expenses underscore the importance of thoroughly understanding the financial implications of crypto investments. The notion that crypto is a cost-free avenue for wealth accumulation is misleading. As with any investment, it's crucial to account for these costs to accurately assess potential returns.

Chapter 8: The Future of Crypto – Fads or the New Normal?

Crypto has generated massive buzz, but what does the future really look like? Is it just another trend that will fade out, or is it here to stay? Right now, no one knows for sure. However, it's worth exploring what might lie ahead for the cryptocurrency market and how it could evolve.

A lot of people see crypto as a way to disrupt traditional finance, but the truth is, it hasn't quite done that yet. Bitcoin, for example, is still far too volatile to be a viable currency for everyday transactions (Zohar). While the concept of decentralized finance (DeFi) is promising, it's still in its infancy. But that doesn't mean we should dismiss it completely. Over time, blockchain technology could play a much bigger role, even beyond cryptocurrency, in fields like supply chain management, voting systems, and even digital identities (Gains, 2020).

There are also efforts to improve the scalability and efficiency of crypto systems. The rise of Ethereum 2.0, which promises to make Ethereum faster and cheaper to use, shows that crypto developers are aware of the limitations and are actively working to improve the infrastructure (Hoffman). But again, the question still remains: will these improvements be enough to push crypto into the mainstream?

As governments around the world begin to regulate crypto more heavily, we could see the market change dramatically. Some people see this as a positive development, as it might make the space more secure and stable. Others worry that over-regulation could stifle innovation and prevent crypto from fulfilling its original promise of decentralization. The balance between regulation and freedom will be a key factor in determining the future of crypto (Kramer).

In the coming years, we may see more institutional investors getting involved. Already, companies like Tesla and MicroStrategy have bought into Bitcoin, signaling that the corporate world is beginning to see crypto as a legitimate asset class (Baca). Even U.S. President Donald Trump went as far as to create a strategic reserve of Bitcoin (Amure). But for it to truly become a long-term investment vehicle, we'll need a lot more stability and clarity in the market.

The future of crypto isn't guaranteed, but it's also not something to ignore. If you're thinking about getting involved, make sure you stay informed and watch the developments closely. The hype might be loud now, but the reality is still unfolding.

Chapter 9: The Eco Impact – Environmental Costs of Crypto

If we are going to talk about crypto's realistic future as a form of real currency, then we definitely have to address the most pressing issues surrounding crypto and that is the environmental impact. While the technology behind cryptocurrencies is often lauded for its innovation, it comes at a high cost to the planet. The energy consumption required to mine and maintain blockchain networks like Bitcoin is staggering, and this has led to significant concerns about the ecological footprint of crypto (Zohar).

Again, like I said, **Bitcoin mining**, requires immense computational power. Mining rigs run 24/7, solving complex mathematical problems to validate transactions and secure the network (Zohar). This process consumes an enormous amount of electricity. In fact, the energy required to mine Bitcoin is comparable to the energy consumption of some small countries (McBride). This puts a serious strain on global energy resources, especially when you consider that much of the electricity used is derived from non-renewable sources (Popper).

The environmental impact doesn't stop there. The **e-waste** generated by mining operations is another major issue. Mining equipment has a relatively short lifespan, and the constant need for newer, more powerful machines creates a massive waste problem (Kollewe). As mining operations scale up, so does the demand for new hardware, adding to the pile of electronic waste.

There's also the issue of **carbon emissions**. The carbon footprint of mining is a significant concern, particularly when crypto mining operations are powered by fossil fuels (Friedman). While some miners are making efforts to transition to renewable energy sources, the fact remains that the vast majority of mining operations still rely on coal and other environmentally harmful energy sources (Kollewe).

However, not all cryptocurrencies are created equal when it comes to sustainability. While Bitcoin's proof-of-work model requires vast energy resources, other cryptocurrencies, like Ethereum, are working on more energy-efficient alternatives. Ethereum's transition to proof-of-stake, which doesn't require mining, is a step in the right direction (Ferdman). But until widespread adoption of more sustainable models occurs, the environmental toll of crypto remains a serious issue.

If you're considering investing in crypto, it's important to be aware of its environmental cost. If sustainability is a concern for you, look into greener alternatives and make sure you're not contributing to the problem. The future of crypto may be digital, but we must ensure that it's not at the cost of our planet.

Chapter 10: The Safer Path Forward – How to Invest Smarter

Now that we've discussed the hype and the hard truth, let's shift the focus to something more constructive: a smarter way to invest in crypto. If you want to dabble in crypto, there are plenty of safer, more reliable paths available. Here's how you might want to go about investing for the first time.

Take It Slow and Learn First

First things first, take it slow. Don't jump in headfirst without a solid plan. Most importantly, educate yourself. Without a doubt, become familiar with who the Federal Reserve is. Understand the tech, the market cycles, and the risks. Without that foundation, you're gambling. If you're not willing to spend the time learning, then crypto may not be the right place to put your money.

Don't Invest In Too Many Coins At Once

I'm sure you've heard all the time about diversifying your investments. Well, throw that logic out when it comes to crypto. With crypto, the key to a successful portfolio is not spreading your money across different types of assets too quickly. Better to start with one coin, to get a feel, now that one coin won't make you rich, but better to start low and slow. This will help you better protect yourself against volatility. I follow the same rule with traditional investments like stocks or bonds. It's not about putting all your eggs in one basket, it's about being smart.

Invest in What You Know

Invest in what you know. This is essential. If you don't understand the technology behind a cryptocurrency you are investing in or you don't grasp the underlying market trends behind it, it's a red flag. The most successful investors focus on what they know and can understand. Take a step back and assess your level of knowledge on the coin. If you're relying on a gut feeling, the next social media trend, or because you heard about it on TV, you're making a risky move. The more informed you are, the better equipped you'll be to make rational decisions rather than emotional ones.

Other Stable Investment Vehicles

Remember, you don't have to invest in crypto to build wealth. There are other, more stable, and often more predictable ways to grow your money. **Precious metals**, like **gold** and **silver**, have stood the test of time as wealth-building vehicles. Yes, they might not come with the same quick rewards that crypto offers, but they are proven. They have real value, and they have a history of steady growth. Stick to the basics, and you'll be much less likely to experience the devastating swings that come with speculative investments.

Patience and Long-Term Strategy

If you're new to investing again, DON'T feel like you have to rush. Take the time to build your knowledge and understand how different markets work. Start small and focus on building a portfolio that aligns with your long-term goals. The best investors are those who start early and stay patient. It's about playing the long game, not trying to make quick, risky bets. By focusing on safer, more predictable investment options, you set yourself up for long-term success, rather than short-term chaos.

Reevaluate Your Financial Goals

Lastly, don't forget to reevaluate your financial goals as you grow. What works for you now may not be the right strategy in a few years. As your financial situation changes, so should your investment strategy. Keep educating yourself, stay aware of market trends, and adjust your portfolio as needed. Building wealth isn't a one-time thing—it's a lifelong process. It requires a commitment to ongoing learning, discipline, and patience. Keep your eyes on your goals and remember that slow, steady growth is often the most reliable way to achieve financial security.

References

Amure, Tobi Opeyemi. *What Trump's Crypto Strategic Reserve Could Mean for Your Investments.* Yahoo! Finance, 4 April 2025. https://finance.yahoo.com/news/trump-crypto-strategic-could-mean-110221437.html (Accessed: April 6, 2025)

Anderson, S., & Kwan, L. (2022). *Crypto and confirmation bias: Why we ignore the risks.* Financial Psychology Press. https://www.financialpsychology.com/crypto-and-confirmation-bias (Accessed: April 6, 2025)

Baca, Michael. *Tesla's Bitcoin Bet: The Risks and Rewards.* Crypto News, 2021. https://www.cryptonews.com/tesla-bitcoin-bet (Accessed: April 6, 2025)

Bankless Times. *Bitcoin Blockchain's Average Transaction Fees Surged 900% In the Last 3 Months to Stand at $15.65.* Bankless Times, 17 May 2023. https://www.banklesstimes.com/news/2023/05/17/bitcoin-blockchains-average-transaction-fees-surged-900percent-in-the-last-3-months-to-stand-at-dollar1565/ (Accessed: April 6, 2025)

Blockaid. (2024, December 19). *More Than Half of Crypto Tokens Debuted in 2024 Were Malicious: Blockaid.* CoinDesk. https://www.coindesk.com/business/2024/12/19/more-than-half-of-crypto-tokens-debuted-in-2024-were-malicious-blockaid (Accessed: April 6, 2025)

Buy Bitcoin Worldwide. *Bitcoin Energy Consumption Statistics.* Buy Bitcoin Worldwide. https://www.buybitcoinworldwide.com/bitcoin-mining-statistics/ (Accessed: April 6, 2025)

CertiK. (2025, January 3). *Phishing Scams Top Crypto Security Threat of 2024 — CertiK.* CoinTelegraph. https://cointelegraph.com/news/phishing-scams-top-crypto-threat-2024-certik (Accessed: April 6, 2025)

Chainalysis. (2025, February 13). *Crypto Crime in 2024 Likely Exceeded $51B, Far Higher Than Reported: Chainalysis.* CoinTelegraph. https://cointelegraph.com/news/crypto-crime-2024-2025-chainalysis (Accessed: April 6, 2025)

CoinDesk. (2022). *Range-Bound Bitcoin Reminds Crypto Twitter of 2018 Lull That Ended With 50% Crash.* CoinDesk. https://www.coindesk.com/markets/2022/10/03/range-bound-bitcoin-reminds-crypto-twitter-of-2018-lull-that-ended-with-50-crash (Accessed: April 6, 2025)

CoinDesk. *Investors Lost Record High $5.6B to Crypto Scams in 2023, FBI Says.* CoinDesk, 9 Sept. 2024. https://www.coindesk.com/policy/2024/09/09/investors-lost-record-high-56b-to-crypto-scams-in-2023-fbi-says (Accessed: April 6, 2025)

CoinMarketCap. (2021). *Bitcoin in 2021: The Highs and Lows.* CoinMarketCap. https://coinmarketcap.com/

academy/article/bitcoin-in-2021-the-highs-and-lows (Accessed: April 6, 2025)

Federal Bureau of Investigation (FBI). (2024, September 9). *Americans Lost $5.6 Billion Last Year in Cryptocurrency Fraud Scams, the FBI Says.* U.S. News & World Report. https://www.usnews.com/news/us/articles/2024-09-09/americans-lost-5-6-billion-last-year-in-cryptocurrency-fraud-scams-the-fbi-says (Accessed: April 6, 2025)

Federal Bureau of Investigation (FBI). *Americans Lost $5.6 Billion Last Year in Cryptocurrency Fraud Scams, FBI Says.* Voice of America News, 9 Sept. 2024. https://www.voanews.com/a/americans-lost-5-6-billion-last-year-in-cryptocurrency-fraud-scams-fbi-says/7777548.html (Accessed: April 6, 2025)

Financial Action Task Force. (2021). *Virtual Assets: Money Laundering and Terrorist Financing Risks.* FATF. https://www.fatf-gafi.org (Accessed: April 6, 2025)

Financial Times. (2021). *Crypto Investment: The Majority Are Losing Money.* Financial Times. https://www.ft.com (Accessed: April 6, 2025)

Foley, S. (2020). *The Crypto Millionaires Who Shaped the Market.* The Financial Times. https://www.ft.com (Accessed: April 6, 2025)

Foley, Emma. *How to Protect Yourself from the Dark Side of Crypto.* The Guardian, 2022. https://www.theguardian.com/crypto-safety (Accessed: April 6, 2025)

Gabbrielli, T. (2021). *FOMO and the Crypto Craze: Emotional Investing in a Volatile Market.* Crypto Press. https://www.cryptopress.com/fomo-crypto (Accessed: April 6, 2025)

Gains, Taylor. *Beyond Crypto: Blockchain's Future in Supply Chain and Governance.* Blockchain Times, 2020. https://www.blockchaintimes.com/beyond-crypto (Accessed: April 6, 2025)

Hobson, E. (2023). *Emotional Investing: How Psychology Drives Crypto Decisions.* Crypto Insight. https://www.cryptoinsight.com/emotional-investing (Accessed: April 6, 2025)

Hughes, Max. *$40 Billion Lost to Crypto Scams in Five Years: The Unseen Dangers.* CryptoInvesting News, 2023. https://www.cryptoinvestingnews.com/crypto-scams (Accessed: April 6, 2025)

Immunefi. *2024 Annual Report*. Immunifi,April 2024. https://immunefi.com/research/(Accessed: April 6, 2025)

Internal Revenue Service. *Taxpayers Need to Report Crypto, Other Digital Asset Transactions on Their Tax Return.* IRS, April 2024. https://www.irs.gov/newsroom/

taxpayers-need-to-report-crypto-other-digital-asset-transactions-on-their-tax-return (Accessed: April 6, 2025)

Kollewe, Julia. *Bitcoin Mining's Environmental Impact: A Problem with No Easy Solution.* BBC News, 24 May 2021. https://www.bbc.com/news/business-57488951 (Accessed: April 6, 2025)

Kramer, Paul. *Balancing Crypto Regulation with Innovation.* Financial Times, 2020. https://www.ft.com/crypto-regulation-innovation (Accessed: April 6, 2025)

Miller, R. (2021). *The Psychology of Risk in Cryptocurrency: Why We Keep Gambling.* FinTech Quarterly, 8(2), 134-145. https://www.fintechquarterly.com/psychology-of-risk (Accessed: April 6, 2025)

McBride, James. *Bitcoin Mining Consumes More Energy Than Some Countries.* CNBC, 19 Nov. 2021. https://www.cnbc.com/2021/11/19/bitcoin-mining-now-uses-more-electricity-than-entire-countries.html (Accessed: April 6, 2025)

Mullins, P. (2023). *Loss Aversion in Crypto: Why Investors Keep Doubling Down.* Financial Behavioral Studies, 30(1), 78-95. https://www.financialbehavioralstudies.com/loss-aversion-crypto (Accessed: April 6, 2025)

Popper, Nathaniel. *How Bitcoin Uses Energy and Why It Matters.* The New York Times, 21 Oct. 2021. https://

www.nytimes.com/2021/10/21/business/energy/bitcoin-mining-eco.html (Accessed: April 6, 2025)

Rosic, A. (2021). *Crypto's Booming Popularity Among Seniors and Retirement Accounts.* Entrepreneur. https://www.entrepreneur.com (Accessed: April 6, 2025)

Smith, Oliver. *Big Crypto Coins Aren't Immune to Hackers: Bitcoin and Ethereum Under Attack.* Bloomberg, 2022. https://www.bloomberg.com/big-crypto-hacks (Accessed: April 6, 2025)

Veritas Protocol. (2024, December 24). *Crypto Scams Surge in 2024, Resulting in $2.3 Billion in Losses.* Veritas Protocol. https://www.veritasprotocol.com/blog/crypto-scams-surge-in-2024-resulting-in-2-3-billion-in-losses (Accessed: April 6, 2025)

YCharts. *Bitcoin Average Transaction Fee Daily Insights: Bitcoin Statistics.* YCharts, 18 Mar. 2025. https://ycharts.com/indicators/bitcoin_average_transaction_fee (Accessed: April 6, 2025)

Zohar, Benjamin. *The Energy Consumption of Bitcoin Mining.* CoinDesk, 13 Oct. 2021. https://www.coindesk.com/markets/2021/10/13/bitcoin-mining-the-most-energy-intensive-process-on-earth/ (Accessed: April 6, 2025)

Zohar, Gilad. *China Tightens Cryptocurrency Regulations: Are Other Countries Following Suit?* Binance, Jan. 2025.

https://www.binance.com/en/square/post/18440584883497
(Accessed: April 6, 2025)

About the Author

Roggie "Raj" Clark is an entrepreneur and a 10-year marketing professional with a proven track record in e-commerce and digital business growth. Having built and managed successful online stores with thousands of sales and consulted for numerous marketing clients, Roggie has mastered the intricacies of online marketing, branding, and consumer behavior. He has also written several popular books on digital marketing, SEO (search engine optimization), and programming (HTML, CSS, and JavaScript).

As a former marketing manager at a fintech company—a role he secured through his own marketing and financial expertise—Roggie gained firsthand experience in financial strategy and wealth-building. This journey inspired him to share insights with amateur investors, helping them save money, make smarter financial decisions, and build long-term wealth. Raj currently lives in Maryland with his sister and niece.

www.ingramcontent.com/pod-product-compliance
Lightning Source LLC
LaVergne TN
LVHW022324200926
848481LV00004B/1421